Save the Planet

Stop Water Waste

Claire Llewellyn

Chrysalis Education

Distributed in the United States by
Smart Apple Media
1980 Lookout Drive
North Mankato, MN 56003

Copyright © Chrysalis Books PLC 2003

ISBN 1-93233-324-X

The Library of Congress control number 2003102560

Editorial Manager: Joyce Bentley
Senior Editor: Sarah Nunn
Design: Stonecastle Graphics Ltd
Illustrations: Paul B. Davies
Picture researcher: Paul Turner

Printed in China

10 9 8 7 6 5 4 3 2 1

Picture credits:
Corbis:
pages 1 © Chinch Gryniewicz; Ecoscene/Corbis, 21 (top) © Corbis.
Garden & Wildlife Matters Photo Library:
pages 5 © M.Collins/Garden Matters (below center), 14 © Wildlife Matters, 15 © Wildlife Matters (top), 16 © Garden Matters (right), 21 (below).
Roddy Paine Photographic Studios:
pages 4, 5 (top), 15 (below), 26-27, 28.
Stonecastle Graphics:
pages 7 (top), 16 (left).
Sylvia Cordaiy Photo Library:
pages 17 (left), 19 (below).

Contents

Water for life

Water! What would we do without it? We wash, cook, and clean with it and drink it by the glass. But none of us should ever take water for granted. Like every animal and plant on Earth, we could not live without it.

Water is a **liquid** with no color, taste, or smell. Yet without it we could not survive.

You need to drink plenty of water to keep your body working properly.

◄ Plants contain a lot of water. All of them need water to grow.

Animals cannot survive without water. They will travel a long way to find it. ▼

The Earth's water

Large parts of the Earth are covered with water, but only some of it is good to drink. The water we use has to be fresh. **Fresh water** is found in rivers and lakes or deep under the ground.

Water covers a lot of the Earth's surface, but sea water is no good to us. It is much too salty to drink.

Fresh water is the only water ▶
we can drink. Some of it is
found in rivers like this.

Fresh water is precious. There is
very little of it on Earth. Most of
the Earth's fresh water is locked
in ice at the Poles. ▼

The water cycle

Water on Earth is always on the move – from the ocean to the air and back to the land. This movement is called the **water cycle**. Earth's water is **recycled** again and again, so it is important to keep it clean.

The Sun heats the water in oceans and lakes.

The water changes into a **gas** called **water vapor** and rises into the air.

The **water vapor** begins to cool as it rises. It changes back into tiny droplets of water and forms clouds.

The water on Earth is **recycled** over and over again.

An oil tanker spills oil into the ocean harming animal and plant life

The water in the clouds falls to land as rain. It fills up rivers that flow to the ocean.

The water cycle is very important for life on Earth.

All of us need clean water. If we **pollute** rivers and oceans, we are poisoning our **water supply**.

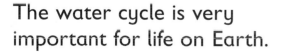

Getting rid of waste

It is easy to pollute the water supply. Many of us do it without even knowing it when we throw things away. Look closely at the picture below. Can you see how everyday waste pollutes rivers and streams?

Rainwater pours into **drains**. This water is clean, and flows into the nearest river.

Our garbage ends up in **landfill sites**. As it rots, it produces nasty liquids that flow into the water deep underground.

Street litter washes down the drain. It ends up in the river.

Garbage is put down the toilet. It goes to **treatment plants**, which cannot cope with it.

Household cleaners are carried to the same treatment plants. They cannot remove all the chemicals.

Oil and paint are being poured down the drain. They will flow into a river, too.

Powders and sprays from the garden wash into drains or soak into the ground.

A better way with waste

We need to try and make less waste. We also need to stop waste polluting our water supply. Can you see ways of doing this in the picture below?

Ponds and rivers are protected and enjoyed.

Waste paper, glass, metals, and plastics are all recycled. This cuts down on garbage.

Litter is put in the trash can. Now it won't wash down the drain.

Diapers and other trash is put in the trash can—not down the toilet.

These cleaning products are kinder to the **environment**.

Home-made **compost** feeds the garden and does not pollute the water supply.

Paint and other dangerous waste is taken to the **waste dump** where it is collected and handled safely.

Factories and farms

Factories and farms pollute our water. Factories sometimes get rid of their waste by pouring it into rivers. Many farmers use powders and sprays on their land. These run into rivers on rainy days, and pollute the water.

The pollution in this water comes from the factory above. It is treating the river like a garbage can.

◄ The sprays and fertilizers that farmers use on their land often end up in streams. This spoils the water.

River water is cleaned before ► it reaches our homes but not everything can be removed.

Freshwater habitats

Rivers and lakes are important **habitats**, and are home to many animals and plants. Water pollution harms habitats. It can poison living things and help to spread disease. The wildlife in these places needs our protection.

Rivers are home to many animals, like these otters, and to plants. They need clean water to survive.

In every habitat big animals feed on smaller animals, and the smallest animals feed on plants. Each **species** is a link in the **food chain**.

When small creatures are poisoned ▶ by pollution, the larger animals that feed on them will be poisoned, too.

▲ Some people help to protect the environment by cleaning rivers and streams.

Pollution in the sea

The oceans are also being polluted—by dirty rivers that flow into it and by ships that dump waste or spill sticky, black oil. Thousands of plants and animals live in the sea. They can all be harmed by dirty water.

When oil is spilled at sea, beaches are damaged or destroyed.

◄ An **oil spill** can kill thousands of creatures. Here, someone is cleaning a seabird, whose feathers have been coated in oil.

Polluted waters wash to every corner of the world. **Coral reefs** are shrinking every year. The tiny animals that build the reefs cannot survive in polluted waters. ▼

More and more water

Every year, we are using more water. Our water comes from **reservoirs** that are filled by rivers and lakes. They are growing shallower, and in time they could dry up. We have to find ways of using less water.

In some parts of the world, farmers are using more water to grow more crops.

In many countries, people have ▶
power showers, washing
machines, and dishwashers.
These things use a lot of water.

Too much water is being taken
from this river. If the river dries
up, the wildlife will not survive. ▼

Using water

A leaking pipe, a running faucet, an overflowing bucket… most of us waste water from time to time. Look carefully at the picture below. Can you see how water is being wasted?

This faucet is dripping. Water is being lost.

A garden sprinkler uses hundreds of gallons of water every hour.

When a hose is used to wash the car, a lot of water runs away wastefully.

A deep bath uses a lot of water.

Do you leave the faucet running while you brush your teeth? That water is running away.

The water is left running until it's cold enough to drink.

The dishwasher and washing machine use a lot of water. But they are running half-empty.

23

A better way of using water

It's not hard to cut down on water waste. Look at the picture below. Can you see how people are saving water? If we save water, our reservoirs will be fuller, and lakes and rivers will be deeper, too.

Don't overwater the garden. Use a watering can when you do.

Only use your dishwasher and washing machine when they are full.

Turn faucets off properly so they do not drip.

A short shower uses less water than a bath.

Turn the faucet off when you wash your hands or brush your teeth.

Collect rainwater in a water barrel and use it to water the garden.

A bottle of water kept in the refrigerator is nice and cold to drink.

Small actions, big results

Is it possible for you to save water and fight water pollution? Of course, it is! And if your small steps are copied by millions of people, the results for the Earth will be huge! Everyone shares the planet and its water supply. Everyone can help to save it.

What would happen if everyone used water carefully?

We would take less water from rivers, lakes, and streams. This would make them deeper, and any pollution in the water would be less strong.

These places would be safer habitats for wildlife.

There would be enough water for everyone to use.

What would happen if everyone stopped polluting rivers and the oceans?

The water in rivers and lakes would be much cleaner. They would make better habitats for animals and plants.

Our drinking water would be safer.

The oceans would be safe for swimmers, wildlife, and underwater habitats, such as coral reefs.

Over to you!

Everyone wants plenty of clean, safe water. Why not try one of the ideas below, and help to stop pollution and water waste?

Talk to your parents about how you could save water at home. Look back at the ideas on pages 24-25.

Think of slogans to explain about pollution ("Don't dump down the drain") or encourage people to save water ("Be Water Wise"). Use them on posters to put up in your school, local library, club house or home.

Try and cut down on trash. For one week, keep a record of everything that's thrown away. What could have been recycled? Pin up your record for the family to see.

Recycle as much waste as you can. Encourage your family to have different containers to sort paper, glass, plastics, cans, and compost.

Encourage your family to buy **organic** foods. Organic farming is kinder to the environment and does not use harmful powders and sprays.

Do a survey to find out how people use water in their homes. Ask your teacher for ideas.

Investigate the way your school uses water. Make and display stickers and posters to encourage people to save water.

Older toilets use a lot of water. In many places you can get a simple device to put inside the tank and save water.

Go pond- or stream-dipping with an adult. This is a good way to check on pollution. The cleaner the water, the more animals you'll find.

Be a 'friend' to local ponds and streams. If you see dead fish, a lot of trash, or colored water, contact the local pwater company.

Join a group in your area that helps to protect the environment. Some of the groups you could try are:

Friends of the Earth *www.foei.org*
Greenpeace *www.greenpeace.org*

Glossary

Compost The crumbly mixture we add to soil to help plants to grow. Compost is made from rotted-down fruit and vegetable peelings.

Coral reef A long line of coral that lies under water in warm, shallow seas.

Drain A pipe that carries water away.

Environment The land, air and sea that make the world around us.

Food chain A way of showing what eats what in a habitat. Some animals feed on plants and are then eaten by other animals.

Fresh water The water that is found in rivers, lakes, and under the ground. Fresh water is not salty, and is good to drink.

Gas A substance like air that is not solid or liquid. Air is made of a mixture of different gases.

Habitat The natural home of an animal or plant.

Landfill site A huge hole in the ground where garbage is buried.

Liquid A substance like water that is runny.

Oil spill A large amount of oil that leaks onto land or into the ocean.

Organic food Foods that have been grown in a natural way that is kinder to the environment.

Pollute To spoil the air, land, or water with harmful things.

Recycle To make something new out of something old.

Reservoir A place where water is stored. Reservoirs look like huge lakes but they are built by people.

Species A kind of animal or plant.

Treatment plant A place where dirty water is cleaned.

Waste dump A place where people take garbage that cannot be put in the trash can.

Water cycle The movement of water from the sea into the air and back to the land.

Water supply All the water that people can use.

Water vapor Tiny droplets of water in air, which are so small you cannot see them.

Index

ML

2/04